Reprint Publishing

For People Who Go For Originals.

www.reprintpublishing.com

THE CONTEST IN AMERICA

By JOHN STUART MILL

REPRINTED FROM FRASER'S MAGAZINE

SECOND EDITION.

BOSTON
LITTLE, BROWN AND COMPANY
MDCCCLXII

RIVERSIDE, CAMBRIDGE:
PRINTED BY H. O. HOUGHTON.

THE CONTEST IN AMERICA.

The cloud which for the space of a month hung gloomily over the civilized world, black with far worse evils than those of simple war, has passed from over our heads without bursting. The fear has not been realized, that the only two first-rate Powers who are also free nations would take to tearing each other in pieces, both the one and the other in a bad and odious cause. For while, on the American side, the war would have been one of reckless persistency in wrong, on ours it would have been a war in alliance with, and, to practical purposes, in defence and propagation of, slavery. We had, indeed, been wronged. We had suffered an indignity, and something more than an indignity, which, not to have resented, would have been to invite a constant succession of insults and injuries from the same and from every other quarter. We could have acted no otherwise than we have done: yet it is impossible to think, without something like a shudder, from what we have escaped. We, the emancipators of the slave — who have wearied every Court and Government in Europe and America with our protests and remonstrances, until we goaded them into at least ostensibly coöperating with us to prevent the enslaving of the negro — we, who for the last half century have spent annual sums, equal to the revenue of a small kingdom, in blockading the African coast, for a cause in which we not only had no interest, but which was contrary to our pecuniary interest, and which many believed would ruin, as many among us still, though erroneously, believe that it has ruined, our colonies, — *we* should have lent a hand to setting up, in one of the most commanding positions of the world, a powerful republic, devoted not only to slavery, but to pro-slavery propagandism — should have helped to give a place in the community of nations to a conspiracy of slave-owners, who have broken their connection with the American Federation on the sole ground, ostentatiously proclaimed, that they thought an attempt would be made to restrain, not slavery itself, but their purpose of spreading slavery wherever migration or force could carry it.

A nation which has made the professions that England has, does not with impunity, under however great provocation, betake itself to frustrating the objects for which it has been calling on the rest of the world to make sacrifices of what they think their interest. At present all the nations of Europe have sympathized with us; have acknowledged that we were injured, and declared with rare unanimity, that we had no choice but to resist, if necessary, by arms. But the consequences of such a war would soon have buried its causes in oblivion. When the new Confederate States, made an independent Power by English help, had begun their crusade to carry negro slavery from the Potomac to Cape Horn; who would then have remembered that England raised up this scourge to humanity not for the evil's sake, but because somebody had offered an insult to her flag? Or even if unforgotten, who would then have felt that such a grievance was a sufficient palliation of the crime? Every reader of a newspaper, to the farthest ends of the earth, would have believed and remembered one thing only — that at the critical juncture which was to decide whether slavery should blaze up afresh with increased vigor or be trodden out — at the moment of conflict between the good and the evil spirit — at the dawn of a hope that the demon might now at last be chained and flung into the pit, England stepped in, and, for the sake of cotton, made Satan victorious.

The world has been saved from this calamity, and England from this disgrace. The accusation would indeed have been a calumny. But to be able to defy calumny, a nation, like an individual, must stand very clear of just reproach in its previous conduct. Unfortunately, we ourselves have given too much plausibility to the charge. Not by anything said or done by us as a Government or as a nation, but by the tone of our press, and in some degree, it must be owned, the general opinion of

English society. It is too true, that the feelings which have been manifested since the beginning of the American contest — the judgments which have been put forth, and the wishes which have been expressed concerning the incidents and probable eventualities of the struggle — the bitter and irritating criticism which has been kept up, not even against both parties equally, but almost solely against the party in the right, and the ungenerous refusal of all those just allowances which no country needs more than our own, whenever its circumstances are as near to those of America as a cut finger is to an almost mortal wound, — these facts, with minds not favorably disposed to us, would have gone far to make the most odious interpretation of the war in which we have been so nearly engaged with the United States, appear by many degrees the most probable. There is no denying that our attitude towards the contending parties (I mean our moral attitude, for politically there was no other course open to us than neutrality) has not been that which becomes a people who are as sincere enemies of slavery as the English really are, and have made as great sacrifices to put an end to it where they could. And it has been an additional misfortune that some of our most powerful journals have been for many years past very unfavorable exponents of English feeling on all subjects connected with slavery: some, probably, from the influences, more or less direct, of West Indian opinions and interests: others from inbred Toryism, which, even when compelled by reason to hold opinions favorable to liberty, is always adverse to it in feeling; which likes the spectacle of irresponsible power exercised by one person over others; which has no moral repugnance to the thought of human beings born to the penal servitude for life, to which for the term of a few years we sentence our most hardened criminals, but keeps its indignation to be expended on " rabid and fanatical abolitionists" across the Atlantic, and on those writers in England who attach a sufficiently serious meaning to their Christian professions, to consider a fight against slavery as a fight for God.

Now, when the mind of England, and it may almost be said, of the civilized part of mankind, has been relieved from the incubus which had weighed on it ever since the *Trent* outrage, and when we are no longer feeling towards the Northern Americans as men feel towards those with whom they may be on the point of struggling for life or death; now, if ever, is the time to review our position, and consider whether we have been feeling what ought to have been felt, and wishing what ought to have been wished, regarding the contest in which the Northern States are engaged with the South.

In considering this matter, we ought to dismiss from our minds, as far as possible, those feelings against the North, which have been engendered not merely by the *Trent* aggression, but by the previous anti-British effusions of newspaper writers and stump orators. It is hardly worth while to ask how far these explosions of ill-humor are anything more than might have been anticipated from ill-disciplined minds, disappointed of the sympathy which they justly thought they had a right to expect from the great anti-slavery people, in their really noble enterprise. It is almost superfluous to remark that a democratic Government always shows worst where other Governments generally show best, on its outside; that unreasonable people are much more noisy than the reasonable; that the froth and scum are the part of a violently fermenting liquid that meets the eyes, but are not its body and substance. Without insisting on these things, I contend, that all previous cause of offence should be considered as cancelled, by the reparation which the American Government has so amply made; not so much the reparation itself, which might have been so made as to leave still greater cause of permanent resentment behind it; but the manner and spirit in which they have made it. These have been such as most of us, I venture to say, did not by any means expect. If reparation were made at all, of which few of us felt more than a hope, we thought that it would have been made obviously as a concession to prudence, not to principle. We thought that there would have been truckling to the newspaper editors and supposed fire-eaters who were crying out for retaining the prisoners at all hazards. We expected that the atonement, if atonement there were, would have been made with reservations, perhaps under protest. We expected that the correspondence would have been spun out, and a trial made to induce England to be satisfied with less; or that there would have been a proposal of arbitration; or that England would have been asked to make concessions in return for justice; or that if submission was made, it would have been made, ostensibly, to the opinions and wishes of Continental Europe. We expected anything, in short, which would have been weak and timid and paltry. The only thing which no one seemed to expect, is what has actually happened. Mr. Lincoln's Government have done none of these things. Like honest men, they have said in direct terms, that our demand was right; that they yielded to it because it was just; that if they themselves had received the same treatment, they would have demanded the same reparation; and that if what seemed to be the American side of a question was not the just side, they would be on the side of justice; happy as they were to find after their resolution had been taken, that it was also the side which America had formerly defended. Is there any one, capable of a moral judgment or feeling, who will say that his opinion of America and American statesmen, is not raised by such an act, done on such grounds? The act itself may have been imposed by the necessity of the circumstances; but the reasons given, the principles of action professed, were their own choice. Putting the worst hypothesis possible, which it would be the height of injustice to entertain seriously, that the concession was really made solely to convenience, and that the profession of regard for justice was hypocrisy, even so, the ground taken, even if insincerely, is the most hopeful sign of the moral state of the American mind which has appeared for many years. That a sense of justice should be the motive which the rulers of a country rely on, to reconcile the public to an unpopular, and what might seem a humiliating act; that the journalists, the orators, many lawyers, the Lower House of Congress, and Mr. Lincoln's own naval secretary, should be told in the face of the world, by their own Government, that they have been giving public thanks, presents of swords, freedom of cities, all manner of heroic honors to the author of an act which, though not so intended, was lawless and wrong, and for which the proper remedy is confession and atonement; that this should be the accepted policy (supposing it to be nothing higher) of a Democratic Republic, shows even unlimited democracy to be a better thing than many Englishmen have lately been in the habit of considering it, and goes some way towards proving that the aberrations even of a ruling multitude are only fatal when the better instructed have not the virtue or the courage to front them boldly. Nor ought it to be forgotten, to the honor of Mr. Lincoln's Government, that in doing what was in itself right, they have done also what was best fitted to allay the animosity which was daily becoming more bitter between the two nations so long as the question remained open. They have put the brand of confessed injustice upon that rankling and vindictive resentment with which the profligate and passionate part of the American press has been threatening us in the event of concession, and which is to be manifested by some dire revenge, to be taken, as they pretend, after the nation is extricated from its present difficulties. Mr. Lincoln has done what depended on him to make this spirit expire with the occasion which raised it up; and we shall have ourselves chiefly to blame if we keep it alive by the further prolongation of that stream of vituperative eloquence, the source of which, even now, when the cause of quarrel has been amicably made up, does not seem to have run dry.[1]

Let us, then, without reference to these jars, or to the declamations of newspaper writers on either side of the Atlantic, examine the American question

---

[1] I do not forget one regrettable passage in Mr. Seward's letter, in which he said that " if the safety of the Union required the detention of the captured persons, it would be the right and duty of this Government to detain them." I sincerely grieve to find this sentence in the dispatch, for the exceptions to the general rules of morality are not a subject to be lightly or unnecessarily tampered with. The doctrine in itself is no other than that professed and acted on by all governments — that self-preservation, in a State, as in an individual, is a warrant for many things which at all other times ought to be rigidly abstained from. At all events, no nation which has ever passed " laws of exception," which ever suspended the Habeas Corpus Act or passed an Alien Bill in dread of a Chartist insurrection, has a right to throw the first stone at Mr. Lincoln's Government.

as it stood from the beginning; its origin, the purpose of both the combatants, and its various possible or probable issues.

There is a theory in England, believed perhaps by some, half believed by many more, which is only consistent with original ignorance, or complete subsequent forgetfulness, of all the antecedents of the contest. There are people who tell us that, on the side of the North, the question is not one of slavery at all. The North, it seems, have no more objection to slavery than the South have. Their leaders never say one word implying disapprobation of it. They are ready, on the contrary, to give it new guarantees; to renounce all that they have been contending for; to win back, if opportunity offers, the South to the Union by surrendering the whole point.

If this be the true state of the case, what are the Southern chiefs fighting about? Their apologists in England say that it is about tariffs, and similar trumpery. *They* say nothing of the kind. They tell the world, and they told their own citizens when they wanted their votes, that the object of the fight was slavery. Many years ago, when General Jackson was President, South Carolina did nearly rebel (she never was near separating) about a tariff; but no other State abetted her, and a strong adverse demonstration from Virginia brought the matter to a close. Yet the tariff of that day was rigidly protective. Compared with that, the one in force at the time of the secession was a free-trade tariff. This latter was the result of several successive modifications in the direction of freedom; and its principle was not protection for protection, but as much of it only as might incidentally result from duties imposed for revenue. Even the Morrill tariff (which never could have been passed but for the Southern secession) is stated by the high authority of Mr. H. C. Carey to be considerably more liberal than the reformed French tariff under Mr. Cobden's treaty; insomuch that he, a Protectionist, would be glad to exchange his own protective tariff for Louis Napoleon's free-trade one. But why discuss, on probable evidence, notorious facts? The world knows what the question between the North and South has been for many years, and still is. Slavery alone was thought of, alone talked of. Slavery was battled for and against, on the floor of Congress and in the plains of Kansas; on the slavery question exclusively was the party constituted which now rules the United States: on slavery Fremont was rejected, on slavery Lincoln was elected; the South separated on slavery, and proclaimed slavery as the one cause of separation.

It is true enough that the North are not carrying on war to abolish slavery in the States where it legally exists. Could it have been expected, or even perhaps desired, that they should? A great party does not change suddenly, and at once, all its principles and professions. The Republican party have taken their stand on law, and the existing constitution of the Union. They have disclaimed all right to attempt anything which that constitution forbids. It does forbid interference by the Federal Congress with slavery in the Slave States; but it does not forbid their abolishing it in the District of Columbia; and this they are now doing, having voted, I perceive, in their present pecuniary straits, a million of dollars to indemnify the slave-owners of the District. Neither did the Constitution, in their own opinion, require them to permit the introduction of slavery into the territories which were not yet States. To prevent this, the Republican party was formed, and to prevent it, they are now fighting, as the slave-owners are fighting to enforce it.

The present government of the United States is not an Abolitionist government. Abolitionists, in America, mean those who do not keep within the constitution; who demand the destruction (as far as slavery is concerned) of as much of it as protects the internal legislation of each State from the control of Congress; who aim at abolishing slavery wherever it exists, by force if need be, but certainly by some other power than the constituted authorities of the Slave States. The Republican party neither aim nor profess to aim at this object. And when we consider the flood of wrath which would have been poured out against them if they did, by the very writers who now taunt them with not doing it, we shall be apt to think the taunt a little misplaced. But though not an Abolitionist party, they are a Free-soil party. If they have not taken arms against slavery, they have against its extension. And they know, as we may know if we please, that this amounts to the same thing. The day when slavery can no longer extend itself, is the day of its doom. The slave-owners know this, and it is the cause of their fury. They know, as all know who have attended to the subject, that confinement within existing limits is its death-warrant. Slavery, under the conditions in which it exists in the States, exhausts even the beneficent powers of nature. So incompatible is it with any kind whatever of skilled labor, that it causes the whole productive resources of the country to be concentrated on one or two products, cotton being the chief, which require, to raise and prepare them for the market, little besides brute animal force. The cotton cultivation, in the opinion of all competent judges, alone saves North American slavery; but cotton cultivation, exclusively adhered to, exhausts in a moderate number of years all the soils which are fit for it, and can only be kept up by travelling farther and farther westward. Mr. Olmsted has given a vivid description of the desolate state of parts of Georgia and the Carolinas, once among the richest specimens of soil and cultivation in the world; and even the more recently colonized Alabama, as he shows, is rapidly following in the same downhill track. To slavery, therefore, it is a matter of life and death to find fresh fields for the employment of slave labor. Confine it to the present States, and the owners of slave property will either be speedily ruined, or will have to find means of reforming and renovating their agricultural system; which cannot be done without treating the slaves like human beings, nor without so large an employment of skilled, that is, of free labor, as will widely displace the unskilled, and so depreciate the pecuniary value of the slave, that the immediate mitigation and ultimate extinction of slavery would be a nearly inevitable and probably rapid consequence.

The Republican leaders do not talk to the public of these almost certain results of success in the present conflict. They talk but little, in the existing emergency, even of the original cause of quarrel. The most ordinary policy teaches them to inscribe on their banner that part only of their known principles in which their supporters are unanimous. The preservation of the Union is an object about which the North are agreed; and it has many adherents, as they believe, in the South generally. That nearly half the population of the Border Slave States are in favor of it is a patent fact, since they are now fighting in its defence. It is not probable that they would be willing to fight directly against slavery. The Republicans well know that if they can reëstablish the Union, they gain everything for which they originally contended; and it would be a plain breach of faith with the Southern friends of the Government, if, after rallying them round its standard for a purpose of which they approve, it were suddenly to alter its terms of communion without their consent.

But the parties in a protracted civil war almost invariably end by taking more extreme, not to say higher grounds of principle, than they began with. Middle parties and friends of compromise are soon left behind ; and if the writers who so severely criticize the present moderation of the Free-soilers are desirous to see the war become an abolition war, it is probable that if the war lasts long enough they will be gratified. Without the smallest pretension to see further into futurity than other people, I at least have foreseen and foretold from the first, that if the South were not promptly put down, the contest would become distinctly an anti-slavery one ; nor do I believe that any person, accustomed to reflect on the course of human affairs in troubled times, can expect anything else. Those who have read, even cursorily, the most valuable testimony to which the English public have access, concerning the real state of affairs in America — the letters of the *Times'* correspondent, Mr. Russell — must have observed how early and rapidly he arrived at the same conclusion, and with what increasing emphasis he now continually reiterates it. In one of his recent letters he names the end of next summer as the period by which, if the war has not sooner terminated, it will have assumed a complete anti-slavery character. So early a term exceeds, I confess, my most sanguine hopes; but if Mr. Russell be right, Heaven forbid that the war should cease sooner; for if it lasts till then, it is quite possible that it will regenerate the American people.

If, however, the purposes of the North may be doubted or misunderstood, there is at least no question as to those of the South. They make no concealment of *their* principles. As long as they were allowed to direct all the policy of the Union; to break through compromise after compromise, encroach step after step, until they reached the pitch of claiming a right to carry slave property into the Free States, and, in opposition to the laws of those States, hold it as property there; so long, they were willing to remain in the Union. The moment a President was elected of whom it was inferred from his opinions, not that he would take any measures against slavery where it exists, but that he would oppose its establishment where it exists not, — that moment they broke loose from what was, at least, a very solemn contract, and formed themselves into a Confederation professing as its fundamental principle not merely the perpetuation, but the indefinite extension of slavery. And the doctrine is loudly preached through the new Republic, that slavery, whether black or white, is a good in itself, and the proper condition of the working classes everywhere.

Let me, in a few words, remind the reader what sort of a thing this is, which the white oligarchy of the South have banded themselves together to propagate and establish, if they could, universally. When it is wished to describe any portion of the human race as in the lowest state of debasement, and under the most cruel oppression, in which it is possible for human beings to live, they are compared to slaves. When words are sought by which to stigmatize the most odious despotism, exercised in the most odious manner, and all other comparisons are found inadequate, the despots are said to be like slave-masters, or slave-drivers. What, by a rhetorical license, the worst oppressors of the human race, by way of stamping on them the most hateful character possible, are said to be, these men, in very truth, are. I do not mean that all of them are hateful personally, any more than all the Inquisitors, or all the buccaneers. But the position which they occupy, and the abstract excellence of which they are in arms to vindicate, is that which the united voice of mankind habitually selects as the type of all hateful qualities. I will not bandy chicanery about the more or less of stripes or other torments which are daily requisite to keep the machine in working order, nor discuss whether the Legrees or the St. Clairs are more numerous among the slave-owners of the Southern States. The broad facts of the case suffice. One fact is enough. There are, Heaven knows, vicious and tyrannical institutions in ample abundance on the earth. But this institution is the only one of them all which requires, to keep it going, that human beings should be burnt alive. The calm and dispassionate Mr. Olmsted affirms that there has not been a single year, for many years past, in which this horror is not known to have been perpetrated in some part or other of the South. And not upon negroes only; the *Edinburgh Review*, in a recent number, gave the hideous details of the burning alive of an unfortunate Northern huckster by Lynch law, on mere suspicion of having aided in the escape of a slave. What must American slavery be, if deeds like these are necessary under it? — and if they are not necessary and are yet done, is not the evidence against slavery still more damning? The South are in rebellion not for simple slavery; they are in rebellion for the right of burning human creatures alive.

But we are told, by a strange misapplication of a true principle, that the South had a *right* to separate; that their separation ought to have been consented to, the moment they showed themselves ready to fight for it; and that the North, in resisting it, are committing the same error and wrong which England committed in opposing the original separation of the thirteen colonies. This is carrying the doctrine of the sacred right of insurrection rather far. It is wonderful how easy and liberal and complying people can be in other people's concerns. Because they are willing to surrender their own past, and have no objection to join in reprobation of their great-grandfathers, they never put themselves the question what they themselves would do in circumstances far less trying, under far less pressure of real national calamity. Would those who profess these ardent revolutionary principles consent to their being applied to Ireland, or India, or the Ionian Islands? How have they treated those who did attempt so to apply them? But the case can dispense with any mere *argumentum ad hominem*. I am not frightened at the word rebellion. I do not scruple to say that I have sympathized more or less ardently with most of the rebellions, successful and unsuccessful, which have taken place in my time. But I certainly never conceived that there was a sufficient title to my sympathy in the mere fact of being a rebel; that the act of taking arms against one's fellow-citizens was so meritorious in itself, was so completely its own justification, that no question need be asked concerning the motive. It seems to me a strange doctrine that the most serious and responsible of all human acts imposes no obligation on those who do it of showing that they have a real grievance; that those who rebel for the power of oppressing others, exercise as sacred a right as those who do the same thing to resist oppression practised upon themselves. Neither rebellion nor any other act which affects the interests of others, is sufficiently legitimated by the mere will to do it. Secession may be laudable, and so may any other kind of insurrection; but it may also be an enormous crime. It is the one or the other, according to the object and the provocation. And if there ever was an object which, by its bare announcement, stamped rebels against a particular community as enemies of mankind, it is the one professed by the South. Their right to separate is the right which Cartouche or Turpin would have had to secede from their respective countries, because the laws of those countries would not suffer them to rob and murder on the highway. The only real difference is that the present rebels are more powerful than Cartouche or Turpin, and may possibly be able to effect their iniquitous purpose.

Suppose, however, for the sake of argument, that the mere will to separate were in this case, or in any case, a sufficient ground for separation, I beg to be informed *whose* will? The will of any knot of men who, by fair means or foul, by usurpation, terrorism, or fraud, have got the reins of government into their hands? If the inmates of Parkhurst Prison were to get possession of the Isle of Wight, occupy its military positions, enlist one part of its inhabitants in their own ranks, set the remainder of them to work in chain gangs, and declare themselves independent, ought their recognition by the British Government to be an immediate consequence? Before admitting the authority of any persons, as organs of the will of the people, to dispose of the whole political existence of a country, I ask to see whether their credentials are from the whole, or only from a part. And first, it is necessary to ask, Have the slaves been consulted? Has *their* will been counted as any part in the estimate of collective volition? They are a part of the population. However natural in the country itself, it is rather cool in English writers who talk so glibly of the ten millions (I believe there are only eight), to pass over the very existence of four millions who must abhor the idea of separation. Remember, *we* consider them to be human beings, entitled to human rights. Nor can it be doubted that the mere fact of belonging to a Union in some parts of which slavery is reprobated, is some alleviation of their condition, if only as regards future probabilities. But even of the white population, it is questionable if there was in the beginning a majority for secession anywhere but in South Carolina. Though the thing was pre-determined, and most of the States committed by their public authorities before the people were called on to vote; though in taking the votes terrorism in many places reigned triumphant; yet even so, in several of the States, secession was carried only by narrow majorities. In some the authorities have not dared to publish the numbers; in some it is asserted that no vote has ever been taken. Further (as was pointed out in an admirable letter by Mr. Carey), the Slave States are intersected in the middle, from their northern frontier almost to the Gulf of Mexico, by a country of free labor — the mountain region of the Alleghanies and their dependencies, forming parts of Virginia, North Carolina, Tennessee, Georgia, and Alabama, in which, from the nature of the climate and of the agricultural and mining industry, slavery to any material extent never did, and never will, exist. This mountain zone is peopled by ardent friends of the Union. Could the Union abandon them, without even an effort, to be dealt with at the pleasure of an exasperated slave-owning oligarchy? Could it abandon the Germans who, in Western Texas, have made so meritorious a commencement of growing cotton on the borders of the Mexican Gulf by free labor? Were the right of the slave-owners to secede ever so clear, they have no right to carry these with them; unless allegiance is a mere question of local proximity, and my next neighbor, if I am a stronger man, can be compelled to follow me in any lawless vagaries I choose to indulge.

But (it is said) the North will never succeed in conquering the South; and since the separation must in the end be recognized, it is better to do at first what must be done at last; moreover, if it did conquer them, it could not govern them when conquered, consistently with free institutions. With no one of these propositions can I agree.

Whether or not the Northern Americans *will* succeed in reconquering the South, I do not affect to foresee. That they *can* conquer it, if their present determination holds, I have never entertained a doubt; for they are twice as numerous, and ten or twelve times as rich. Not by taking military possession of their country, or marching an army through it, but by wearing them out, exhausting their resources, depriving them of the comforts of life, encouraging their slaves to desert, and excluding them from communication with foreign countries. All this, of course, depends on the supposition that the North does not give in first. Whether they will persevere to this point, or whether their spirit, their patience, and the sacrifices they are willing to make, will be exhausted before reaching it, I cannot tell. They may, in the end, be wearied into recognizing the separation. But to those who say that because this may have to be done at last, it ought to have been done at first, I put the very serious question — On what terms? Have they ever considered what would have been the meaning of separation if it had been assented to by the Northern States when first demanded? People talk as if separation meant nothing more than the independence of the seceding States. To have accepted it under that limitation would have been, on the part of the South, to give up that which they have seceded expressly to preserve. Separation, with them, means at least half the Territories; including the Mexican border, and the consequent power of invading and overrunning Spanish America for the purpose of planting there the "peculiar institution" which even Mexican civilization has found too bad to be endured. There is no knowing to what point of degradation a country may be driven in a desperate state of its affairs; but if the North *ever*, unless on the brink of actual ruin, makes peace with the South, giving up the original cause of quarrel, the freedom of the Territories; if it resigns to them when out of the Union that power of evil which it would not grant to retain them in the Union — it will incur the pity and disdain of posterity. And no one can suppose that the South would have consented, or in their present temper ever will consent, to an accommodation on any other terms. It will require a succession of humiliation to bring them to that. The necessity of reconciling themselves to the confinement of slavery within its existing boundaries, with the natural consequence, immediate mitigation of slavery, and ultimate emancipation, is a lesson which they are in no mood to learn from anything but disaster. Two or three defeats in the field, breaking their military strength, though not followed by an invasion of their territory, may possibly teach it to them. If so, there is no breach of charity in hoping that this severe schooling may promptly come. When men set themselves up, in defiance of the rest of the world, to do the devil's work, no good can come of them until the world has made them feel that this work cannot be suffered to be done any longer. If this knowledge does not come to them for several years, the abolition question will by that time have settled itself. For assuredly Congress will very soon make up its mind to declare all slaves free who belong to persons in arms against the Union. When that is done, slavery, confined to a minority, will soon cure itself; and the pecuniary value of the negroes belonging to loyal masters will probably not exceed the amount of compensation which the United States will be willing and able to give.

The assumed difficulty of governing the Southern States as free and equal commonwealths, in case of their return to the Union, is purely imaginary. If brought back by force, and not by voluntary compact, they will return without the Territories, and without a Fugitive Slave Law. It may be assumed that in that event the victorious party would make the alterations in the Federal Constitution which are necessary to adapt it to the new circumstances, and which would not infringe, but strengthen, its democratic principles. An article would have to be inserted prohibiting the extension of slavery to the Territories, or the admission into the Union of any new Slave State. Without any other guarantee, the rapid formation of new Free States would ensure to freedom a decisive and constantly increasing majority in Congress. It would also be right to abrogate that bad provision of the Constitution (a necessary compromise at the time of its first establishment) whereby the slaves, though reckoned as citizens in no other respect, are counted, to the extent of three fifths of their number, in the estimate of the population for fixing the number of representatives of each State in the Lower House of Congress. Why should the masters have members in right of their human chattels, any more than of their oxen and pigs? The President, in his Message, has already proposed that this salutary reform should be effected in the case of Maryland, additional territory, detached from Virginia, being given to that State as an equivalent: thus clearly indicating the policy which he approves, and which he is probably willing to make universal.

As it is necessary to be prepared for all possibilities, let us now contemplate another. Let us suppose the worst possible issue of this war — the one apparently desired by those English writers whose moral feeling is so philosophically indifferent between the apostles of slavery and its enemies. Suppose that the North should stoop to recognize the new Confederation on its own terms, leaving it half the Territories, and that it is acknowledged by Europe, and takes its place as an admitted member of the community of nations. It will be desirable to take thought beforehand what are to be our own future relations with a new Power, professing the principles of Attila and Genghis Khan as the foundation of its Constitution. Are we to see with indifference its victorious army let loose to propagate their national faith at the rifle's mouth through Mexico and Central America? Shall we submit to see fire and sword carried over Cuba and Porto Rico, and Hayti and Liberia conquered and brought back to slavery? We shall soon have causes enough of quarrel on our own account. When we are in the act of sending an expedition against Mexico to redress the wrongs of private British subjects, we should do well to reflect in time that the President of the new Republic, Mr. Jefferson Davis, was the original inventor of repudiation. Mississippi was the first State which repudiated, Mr. Jefferson Davis was Governor of Mississippi, and the Legislature of Mississippi had passed a Bill recognizing and providing for the debt, which Bill Mr. Jefferson Davis vetoed. Unless we abandon the principles we have for two generations consistently professed and acted on, we should be at war with the new Confederacy within five years about the African slave-trade. An English Government will hardly be base enough to recognize them, unless they accept all the treaties by which America is at present bound; nor, it may be hoped, even if *de facto* independent, would they be admitted to the courtesies of diplomatic intercourse, unless they granted in the most explicit manner the right of search. To allow the slave-ships of a Confederation formed for the extension of slavery to come and go free, and unexamined, between America and the African coast, would be to renounce even the pretence of attempting to protect Africa against the man-stealer, and abandon that Continent to the horrors, on a far larger scale, which were practised before Granville Sharp and Clarkson were in existence. But even if the right of intercepting their slavers were acknowledged by treaty, which it never would be, the arrogance of the Southern slave-holders would not long submit to its exercise. Their pride and self-conceit, swelled to an inordinate height by their successful struggle, would defy the power of England as they had already successfully defied that of their Northern countrymen. After our people by their cold disapprobation, and our press by its invective, had combined with their own difficulties to damp the spirit of the Free States, and drive them to submit and make peace, we should have to fight the Slave States ourselves at far greater disadvantages, when we should no longer have the wearied and exhausted North for an ally. The time might come when the barbarous and barbarizing Power, which we by our moral support had helped into existence, would require a general crusade of civilized Europe, to extinguish the mischief which it had allowed, and we had aided, to rise up in the midst of our civilization.

For these reasons I cannot join with those who cry Peace, peace. I cannot wish that this war should not have been engaged in by the North, or that being engaged in, it should be terminated on any conditions but such as would retain the whole of the Territories as free soil. I am not blind to the possibility that it may require a long war to lower the arrogance and tame the aggressive ambition of the slave-owners, to the point of either returning to the Union, or consenting to remain out of it with their present limits. But war, in a good cause, is not the greatest evil which a nation can suffer. War is an ugly thing, but not the ugliest of things: the decayed and degraded state of moral and patriotic feeling which thinks nothing *worth* a war, is worse. When a people are used as mere human instruments for firing cannon or thrusting bayonets, in the service and for the selfish purposes of a master, such war degrades a people. A war to protect other human beings against tyrannical injustice; a war to give victory to their own ideas of right and good, and which is their own war, carried on for an honest purpose by their free choice — is often the means of their regeneration. A man who has nothing which he is willing to fight for, nothing which he cares more about than he does about his personal safety, is a miserable creature, who has no chance of being free, unless made and kept so by the exertions of better men than himself. As long as justice and injustice have not terminated *their* ever renewing fight for ascendancy in the affairs of mankind, human beings must be willing, when need is, to do battle for the one against the other. I am far from saying that the present struggle, on the part of the Northern Americans, is wholly of this exalted character; that it has arrived at the stage of being altogether a war for justice, a war of principle. But there was from the beginning, and now is, a large infusion of that element in it; and this is increasing, will increase, and if the war lasts, will in the end predominate. Should that time come, not only will the greatest enormity which still exists among mankind as an institution, receive far earlier its *coup de grâce* than there has ever, until now, appeared any probability of; but in effecting this the Free States will have raised themselves to that elevated position in the scale of morality and dignity, which is derived from great sacrifices consciously made in a virtuous cause, and the sense of an inestimable benefit to all future ages, brought about by their own voluntary efforts.

THE END.

Reprint Publishing

FOR PEOPLE WHO GO FOR ORIGINALS.

This book is a facsimile reprint of the original edition. The term refers to the facsimile with an original in size and design exactly matching simulation as photographic or scanned reproduction.

Facsimile editions offer us the chance to join in the library of historical, cultural and scientific history of mankind, and to rediscover.

The books of the facsimile edition may have marks, notations and other marginalia and pages with errors contained in the original volume. These traces of the past refers to the historical journey that has covered the book.

ISBN 978-3-95940-176-0

Facsimile reprint of the original edition
Copyright © 2016 Reprint Publishing
All rights reserved.

www.reprintpublishing.com

www.ingramcontent.com/pod-product-compliance
Lightning Source LLC
Chambersburg PA
CBHW061518040426
42450CB00008B/1679